The Boy with a SLING

1 SAMUEL 16:1—18:5 FOR CHILDREN

Written by
Mary Warren

Illustrated by
Sally Mathews

Long before
Mary or Joseph or Jesus were born,
God said to Samuel, His priest,
"Put oil in your horn,
and go now and find
the Bethlehem boy I have in mind
to be king of my people some day."

ARCH Books

© 1965 CONCORDIA PUBLISHING HOUSE, ST. LOUIS, MISSOURI

LIBRARY OF CONGRESS CATALOG CARD NO. 65-15143
MANUFACTURED IN THE UNITED STATES OF AMERICA
ALL RIGHTS RESERVED
ISBN 0-570-06012-5

It was to the home of Jesse
that Samuel went.
After meeting and greeting his sons,
he asked:
"Are there more?"
And so Jesse sent
to the fields for his youngest,
David the shepherd boy,
handsome and strong.

God said to Samuel:
"You are looking for one to be king —
this is he!
Take holy oil, anoint him for Me!"

Nobody knew
except God and His holy man, Samuel,
what this would do.
Alone on the hills, he had to keep
lions and bears from stealing his sheep,
and the Spirit of God gave him such
courage and might
that the wildest of creatures
he dared to fight!

There was at this time a long war.
The Philistine army
and the Israelites, under King Saul,
camped on two mountains.

Each morning a Philistine giant,
Goliath of Gath,
came down in the Valley of Elah to call
"Is any man there
who will fight against me?
I shall chop off his head
and cut up his body like bread
to toss to the beasts
and the birds!
WHO WILL DARE?"

Goliath the giant put fear
in each Israelite heart with his shout.
His brass armor clinked; his long spear
made even the bravest men doubt
that any could fight him and win.

One day the shepherd boy, David, came
with cheese and some bread
for his brothers
who fought in Saul's army.
Like the others, they ran
when Goliath came down.

When David saw this,
he said with a frown:
"Goliath makes fun of our God!
Does no one believe that the Lord
takes care of His armies in need?

"I will fight this giant myself!"

King Saul heard of David's brave words.
He sent for the boy and he smiled.
"You are hardly more than a child!
Goliath knows all about war!
What are *you* offering for?"

Said David: "Out in the field
when either a lion or bear
tried to steal my father's young sheep,
my God helped me fight with him there.
I know in this battle God will
shield and deliver me still!"

Saul put his armor on David:
"Here is my coat of mail . . .
my helmet . . . my very own sword.
Go! In the name of the Lord!"

But Saul's armor was heavy; he fell.
"I cannot wear them, O King!
I am used to only a sling!"

With his sling and his shepherd's crook
David stopped to search at the brook
for some stones.
With these in his bag, he went on
to the place where Goliath of Gath
made the Israelites tremble in fear.
"Who is there?" roared Goliath.

His shield bearer stood before him, but he
was still able to see
David the shepherd boy. And with a sneer
and a laugh that was cruel,
Goliath drew near.

"Why do you pick
such a boy for this fight?
Am I but a dog to be chased with a stick?
Come! I will throw all your bones
to the birds of the air
and the beasts of the field!"

David reached for his stones.
"Your spear is sharp and long and strong;
your shield is great and heavy too.
There is one reason that I came.
You mock the Lord and . . . in His name
I have power to conquer you!"

David's hand dipped in his bag.
Before Goliath had time to see
he put a stone in his sling and — WHEE!

It hit the Philistine in the head;

he staggered, then fell forward —

Goliath was DEAD.

David ran with a glorious shout
and took the giant's heavy sword
and cut his head off. Soon the word
spread through the Philistine camp.
The men raced hard to get away
but the Israelites were close behind
and many Philistines died that day.

Triumphantly they marched to bring
the battle news and Goliath's head
to Saul, the waiting king, who said:
"Your strength from God, O David, wins
Israel this victory;
my army needs such bravery!"

From that day on young David stayed
at court with Saul, who knew he'd need
a captain who was strong to lead
his men in other battles too.

This army training helped him grow
to be, in time, God's chosen king —
he who once had been a boy
who killed a giant with a sling!

Dear Parents:

The story of David and Goliath is so loved by all children because here a "big bully," the giant Goliath, gets outsmarted and defeated by the "little guy," David.

In a way this story stands for the entire history of the People of God. God surprises us again and again by the instruments He chooses: the little nation Israel, the timid Moses (Exodus 4:10-16), the young shepherd boy David, the little nobody Mary, the simple fishermen, the unimpressive speaker Paul (1 Corinthians 2:1-5). God gives His Spirit and power to the least likely people and changes the lives of men and of nations through them.

It is really not David or Moses or any of the important figures of the Bible who is the "hero," but God, who saves His People through them, who "resists the proud" and is the Champion of the oppressed. It is He who gives power to the powerless, wisdom to the simple, and opens up new possibilities where men see only a dead end.

Will you help your child understand this as you talk over the story, and lead him to believe it by the way you yourself deal with the pressures and anxieties of life?

THE EDITOR